Contents

INTRODUCTION	4
ARIES	9
TAURUS	19
GEMINI	29
CANCER	39
LEO	49
VIRGO	59
LIBRA	69
SCORPIO	79
SAGITTARIUS	89
CAPRICORN	99
AQUARIUS	109
PISCES	119

Introduction

Uhat Is Astrology?

Since ancient times, people have looked to the skies in search of meaning. Today, astrologers study the movements and positions of celestial bodies—the Sun, Moon, planets, and stars—and use this information to uncover insights about your personality and life.

WHAT'S YOUR SIGN?

The zodiac is a belt of sky that contains twelve famous groups of stars, or constellations. Over the course of one year, the Sun appears to move around the zodiac, passing through a different constellation each month. (Of course, the Earth is actually moving around the Sun!) Your Sun sign is the constellation that the Sun was in when you were born.

In astrology, the Sun symbolizes your identity—the parts of yourself that you shine out to the world! Understanding your Sun sign, and its influence on your personality, relationships, work, and wellbeing, can give you an insight into what makes you special. To discover your Sun sign (also called your star sign), all you need is your birth date.

Birth date	Sun sign
March 21–April 20	Aries
April 21–May 20	Taurus
May 21–June 21	Gemini
June 22–July 22	Cancer
July 23–August 23	Leo
August 24–September 22	Virgo
September 23–October 22	Libra
October 23–November 21	Scorpio
November 22–December 19	Sagittarius
December 20–January 19	Capricorn
January 20–February 19	Aquarius
February 20–March 20	Pisces

Cusp dates

If you were born on a day either side of the dates shown for your zodiac sign, you were born on the "cusp" of two signs. The exact time of the Sun's entry into each zodiac sign varies slightly every year. You can check online to discover the exact moment the Sun moved into each zodiac sign in the year you were born.

Aries
March 21– April 20

All About Aries

SYMBOL: THE RAM
ELEMENT: FIRE △
RULER: MARS

The constellation of Aries

As the first sign of the zodiac, you are a natural leader who lets nothing get in your way. You prefer taking action over talking or thinking, and your reactions are lightning fast! This can make you a little impatient with people who can't keep up—you just don't understand why anyone wants to waste time discussing details. Anger can sometimes bubble up to the surface, but luckily your frustration is usually explosive and short-lived.

Brave and uncomplicated

You're not frightened to speak up about how you feel. You may have a reputation for being tactless, but you're also admired for your outspoken nature. You say what you are thinking and secretly wish that everyone else would do the same. Honesty is your superpower, and dishonesty in others leaves you confused.

Spontaneous spender

In your world, cash goes out as fast as it comes in. You're an impulsive spender, which means that if you see something that makes you happy, you treat yourself. You would rather splash the cash all at once—and have nothing to spend for a little while—than say no.

Fast and furious

You achieve your goals fast, fearlessly, and furiously, but you may run out of steam toward the end of more complicated projects. You prefer to charge in, do your thing, and leave. This is great for dramatic effect but not for tasks that require patience or stamina. Household chores are unlikely to be your priority …

ARIES AND RELATIONSHIPS

You're open and honest about your feelings, which makes you an exciting person to be around. You're not slow to put yourself forward, and you usually know what to do to impress your crush. However, although you have complete faith in yourself, it can take you a little while to feel sure about anyone else. You may experience a few ups and downs before finding the person who's right for you, but the universe knows you can handle it. After all, where's the challenge in finding true love right away?

Perfect relationships

- You need to be around people who can match your energy and won't be afraid of a challenge.
- You don't like mind games and refuse to waste time on people who aren't interested in you.
- You hate feeling vulnerable and only let your guard down with people you trust.
- If someone breaks your heart, your grief is real—but it doesn't take you too long to get over it.

GOOD MATCH
- Aries
- Leo
- Libra

STEER CLEAR
- Virgo
- Taurus
- Cancer

ARIES AT WORK

You love to lead, and you play to win—skills that make you a legendary boss, and ultimately that's where you're heading! However, to get the top position, you need to master a few workplace habits. You enthusiastically plunge into new projects … but with a little more preparation, you will be able to finish them, too! Your energy is admirable.

Not everyone is as ready as you to take on difficult challenges, and your ideas are always appreciated. You're never stumped for an answer and are often the one to kick off brainstorming sessions.

Inspirational Aries

- **Emma Watson—Actor**
- **Saoirse Ronan—Actor**
- **Lady Gaga—Musician and actor**
- **Vincent van Gogh—Artist**
- **Lil Nas X—Musician**
- **Alek Wek—Model and designer**

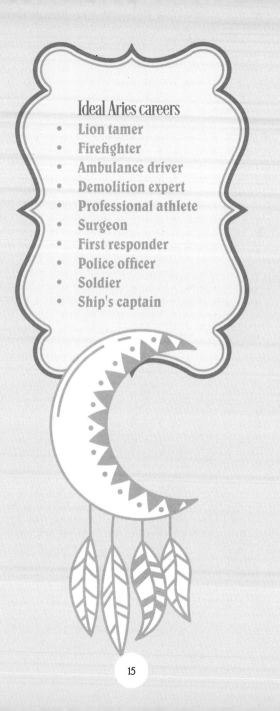

Ideal Aries careers

- Lion tamer
- Firefighter
- Ambulance driver
- Demolition expert
- Professional athlete
- Surgeon
- First responder
- Police officer
- Soldier
- Ship's captain

ARIES AT PLAY

You're a natural at games and sports, and you enjoy setting yourself goals and smashing through your targets. Most other zodiac signs can't match your physical abilities. You're usually a fast mover but more of a sprinter than a long-distance runner—you're happy to put in lots of effort, but you can easily get bored. Because you use up so much energy, it's important that you balance activities with plenty of sleep.

Food and drink

- As a Fire sign, you enjoy hot, spicy food and are not a particularly fussy eater.
- Fast food works for you—as long as you balance it with lively activity.
- If you could, you'd eat out at a different place every day.
- You're more into street food than candlelit dinners, and you love buffets.

Get moving

You need space around you and plenty of fresh air. You don't care if the weather's bad. Exercising in snow, wind, and rain just adds to the challenge for you. You're not usually a team player, preferring the freedom of going it alone, unless we're talking about sports! You excel at physically demanding team sports and are usually a key player.

Taurus
April 21–
May 20

ALL ABOUT TAURUS

SYMBOL: THE BULL
ELEMENT: EARTH ▽
RULER: VENUS

The constellation of Taurus

You are the strong, silent rock of the zodiac—trustworthy and unchanging; without your strength, everything else collapses. Taurus is ruled by Venus, giving you good looks and an easy charm. You work toward your goals slowly and with determination. Patience is your superpower. When you know something is right for you, you'll accept that it may take a long time to get there. But you know with some certainty that you will.

Honest and hardworking

Taurus has a knack for accumulating money, but you're not a workaholic. You work for money to buy beautiful stuff! Some people think you are lazy, but they are mistaken. You know when to work and when to relax. You like to do things properly and keep going even when times are hard.

Staying in

You adore home comforts and good food. Your home is your castle, where you feel most content. An evening spent in your fluffy robe, surrounded by your family on a plumped-up sofa with a delicious home-cooked meal, will never be unappealing.

Serene or raging bull?

On the surface, it may look like nothing ever bothers you. This often makes people think that you are emotionless. Wrong! Earth signs can get very emotional, it just takes you longer to get there. Bulls know that when they charge, they lose it—and this can be devastating for everyone involved.

TAURUS AND RELATIONSHIPS

Your easy-going nature, sense of fun, and good looks draw people to you. You don't fall for people easily, but when you do, you are a loyal friend or partner with an inner confidence that can be irresistible. Once you feel secure in a relationship, you shower the people you love with affection and like to spend lots of your time in their company. If you fear that they're spending more time with other people, you get jealous ... But it's only natural for the zodiac sign connected with possessions to be a little clingy with the most important thing in their life.

Perfect relationships

- You respect the conventional route to romance, such as candlelit dinners, flowers, and walks at sunset.
- You like people who look, smell, and sound good, too. A person's voice can be a deal-breaker for you.
- Good cooks definitely have a head start in the competition to catch your eye!
- Taurus is a money-oriented sign, and a partner with a healthy bank balance makes you feel secure.

GOOD MATCH
- Capricorn
- Cancer
- Scorpio

STEER CLEAR
- Sagittarius
- Gemini
- Aquarius

TAURUS AT WORK

You're one of the most hardworking signs of the zodiac—
and if you make promises, they'll be delivered. You're not
always the speediest, but you take pride in your work, which
is usually of excellent quality. Not a huge fan of change,
Taurus is the sign most likely to stay in the same job for a
long time. You find methodical and repetitive work rather
comforting, but that doesn't mean you're not creative. Ruled
by artistic Venus, you're a patient soul who can spend weeks
perfecting a painting or composing a concerto.

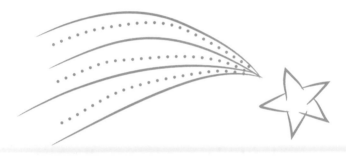

Inspirational Taurus

- **Dwayne Johnson—Actor**
- **William Shakespeare—Writer**
- **Adele—Musician**
- **Lizzo—Musician**
- **Florence Nightingale—Nurse and activist**
- **Joe Keery—Actor**

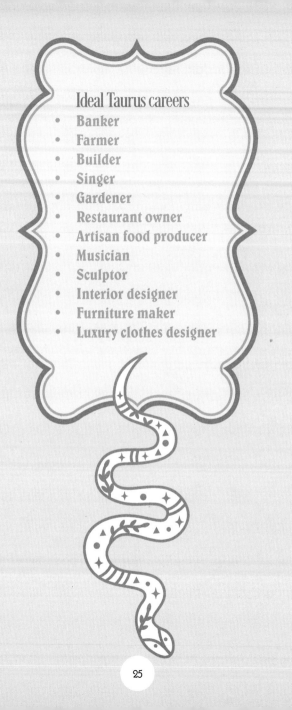

Ideal Taurus careers

- Banker
- Farmer
- Builder
- Singer
- Gardener
- Restaurant owner
- Artisan food producer
- Musician
- Sculptor
- Interior designer
- Furniture maker
- Luxury clothes designer

TAURUS AT PLAY

A true Taurus is a slow, purposeful mover who has one speed—their own. You hate being rushed into anything! If you're being hassled to get going with something, you'll simply stop in your tracks. You win at life through force of will. Robust and strong, you are usually in good health. You're not really athletic, but you do have plenty of stamina and determination. Taurus has turned lounging into an art form ... your ideal home is filled with comfy chairs, flattering lighting, candles, and soft music.

Food and drink

- For Taurus, food is an all-consuming experience. Food takes you to another world!
- Your taste buds are sharp, and you thoroughly enjoy good food.
- You may find yourself drawn to starchy food—and love all things made out of potatoes!
- Eating involves all the senses—it must look as good as it tastes.

Get moving

You prefer a predictable routine to fit into your well-ordered lifestyle, but getting sweaty and out of breath is all a bit too uncomfortable for you. The gym might not be your natural home, but enjoying being outside in the fresh air is a different story.

Gemini

May 21–June 21

ALL ABOUT GEMINI

SYMBOL: THE TWINS
ELEMENT: AIR △
RULER: MERCURY

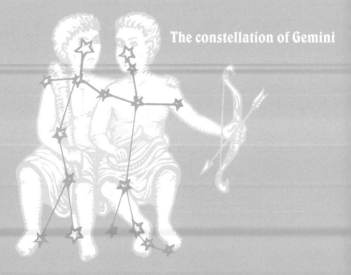

The constellation of Gemini

Intelligent, adaptable, and bubbly, you're the cleverest zodiac sign. Your moods are as changeable as the weather, flitting from blue skies to rain clouds in a moment. You adapt to the situations you experience, finding it easy to blend in and agree with whoever you're with. But a focused Gemini is a genius. When your mind is engaged, you get through your work twice as fast as everyone else—and the results are always thoughtful and entertaining.

Sensitive soul

You appear sunny and bubbly on the outside, even if you're in a bleak mood underneath. You don't mind talking about your bad feelings, but you're not interested in finding out the source of the pain. Your emotional reactions can be as mysterious to you as they are to others!

Dual nature

Ruled by Mercury, the communications planet, you like to know something about everything. Whether it's physics or pottery, you have a thirst for knowledge and new experiences. The flip side is that you live so much in your mind that you can forget to return messages, turn up late, and sometimes just stop halfway through sentences ...

Restless curiosity

A bored Gemini is dangerous. Boredom can bring out your "dark twin," who will say anything to get a reaction. What you see as harmless chatter might actually be unkind, exaggerated, or untrue. This doesn't mean you can't be kind or caring—in fact, your ability to see things from all sides makes you sensitive to other people's points of view.

GEMINI AND RELATIONSHIPS

You're one of the friendliest signs of the zodiac, and you fall a little bit in love with anyone and everyone when you first get to know them. You're drawn to new people in a way that no other zodiac sign is, and you typically experience a few romances before you settle down. Romantic love brings happiness—or tricky feelings if your partner upsets you. When you're unsure of what's causing difficult feelings, your mood can quickly change. To bond with other people, you must first bond with yourself—then your relationships will go from strength to strength.

Perfect relationships?

- You like people who have a lifestyle very different to your own.
- A bright intellect and enthusiasm for life will keep you coming back for more.
- Your friends and partners must have a sense of fun. You'll feel bored with anyone who takes you too seriously.
- You love talking—it's your superpower! You are only content when the people around you know how to communicate.

GOOD MATCH
- Aquarius
- Pisces
- Leo

STEER CLEAR
- Scorpio
- Gemini
- Taurus

GEMINI AT WORK

As a flexible Air sign, you adapt easily to new situations. You're a quick, logical decision-maker who instinctively knows what to do. You're not interested in traditional ways of doing things or how things may have been done in the past. You enjoy working in large teams with a varied group of people. If you become bored at work, you'll be easily distracted. Your "dark twin" will appear, and you may start to cause mischief, just for your own amusement.

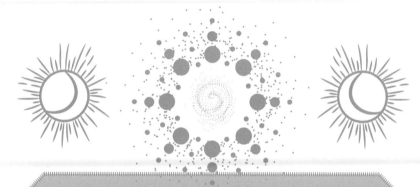

Inspirational Gemini

- **Venus Williams—Tennis player**
- **Anne Frank—Writer**
- **Marilyn Monroe—Actor**
- **Tom Holland—Actor**
- **Aly Raisman—Gymnast and activist**
- **Awkwafina—Comedian, musician, and actor**

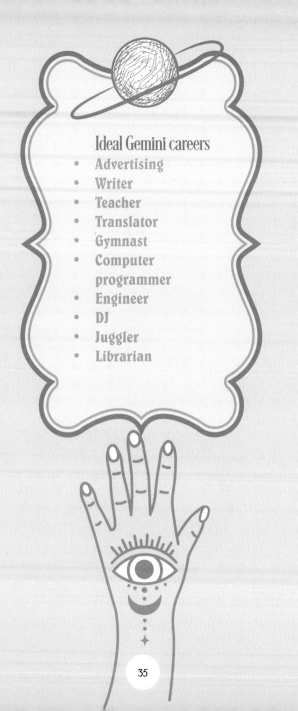

Ideal Gemini careers

- Advertising
- Writer
- Teacher
- Translator
- Gymnast
- Computer programmer
- Engineer
- DJ
- Juggler
- Librarian

GEMINI AT PLAY

As an Air sign, you are never still and crave plenty of variety to keep you feeling active, positive, and content. An unusually speedy walker, you often get to your destination faster on foot than using public transportation. Exploring new restaurants, cafés, and market stalls is just as interesting to you as the food on offer. Watching cooking shows to learn about new ways to prepare meals can satisfy your appetite almost as much as preparing the food itself.

Food and drink

- Eating the same food at the same time every day is boring for a Gemini. You prefer to eat little and often.
- You tend to be more of a picker than a heavy meal kind of person.
- You have a taste for the unusual. If someone offered you an artichoke sandwich, you'd probably give it a try!
- Since you burn so much energy, you need to drink lots of water.

Get moving

When you need a workout, you are more interested in intense, short bursts of activity such as spin classes or interval training. What you lack in strength and stamina, you make up for in agility and flexibility. Long hikes and planned tours aren't really your idea of fun, since you get a little impatient and start looking for the next challenge.

Cancer

June 22–
July 22

All about Cancer

SYMBOL: THE CRAB
ELEMENT: WATER ▽
RULED BY: THE MOON

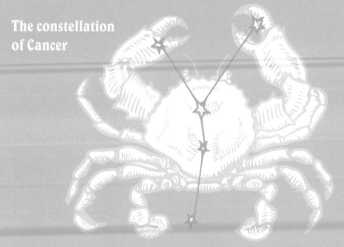

The constellation of Cancer

Just like your zodiac symbol, the Crab, your tough outer personality protects the softer inner you. You don't need to be the focus of attention, you just want to be left alone to get going with things. You can be a little shy with people you don't know, but that's just because you're such a giving person. Most people are nowhere near as tuned into the world of feelings as you. Once you let people into your enormous heart, you don't know how to give them up. Thank goodness you understand that laughter can take the sting out of emotionally tense situations!

Pinch where it hurts

If you're really hurt by someone else's actions, you retreat into your shell. The silent treatment usually gets your message across! But if a loved one has angered you, it's a different story. It happens rarely, but when you take revenge, you use your claws to pinch where it will hurt the most.

Clinging to the past

A lover of tradition, antiques, and history, you attach sentimental value to old photographs, gifts, and even clothes. You find comfort in these old things and guard them carefully. Perhaps you no longer see these things as clutter but rather as more of an extension of your own protective shell.

Caring soul

You are a great caregiver, and your instincts are to love, nurture, and protect. You're a wonderful listener. You don't question or judge what happened—if someone you love is in trouble, that's enough. You'll offer the coat off your back to help, with no thought for your own needs.

CANCER AND RELATIONSHIPS

When you like someone, it often scares you a little. Your first instinct might be to hide and worry about all the things that could go wrong! But you, more than any other zodiac sign, have the emotional capacity needed to navigate the human heart. Some may say that you are overly dramatic or too needy, but you understand what a big deal giving even a tiny piece of your heart is—because the rest of your heart is usually close behind.

Perfect relationships?

- You're one of the most romantic zodiac signs. When you really like someone, you place them at the heart of your universe.
- Emotional compatibility is important to you. You want to share every emotion with the people you love.
- Domestic bliss is your aim, and you love the idea of setting up a home and family one day.
- You expect to be able to talk to the people you love about everything—and expect the same from them.

GOOD MATCH
- Taurus
- Capricorn
- Scorpio

STEER CLEAR
- Aquarius
- Sagittarius
- Libra

CANCER AT WORK

You're better with money than most, and you like to feel secure. You're a saver at heart, and the thought of not having a little spare cash in the bank is one of your biggest anxieties. You're not frightened of taking on jobs that others would turn their noses up at, as long as there's a paycheck at the end of it. It's this dedication that causes you to be passionate about helping people less fortunate than yourself. Behind your shy appearance beats the heart of a leader! Gentle but firm, you often rise to the top of your profession.

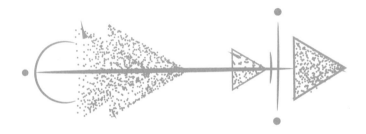

Inspirational Cancer

- Ariana Grande—Musician
- Nelson Mandela—Politician
- Selena Gomez—Actor and musician
- Malala Yousafzai—Writer and activist
- Alan Turing—Computer programmer
- Jaden Smith—Actor and musician

Ideal Cancer careers

- Nurse
- Nursery teacher
- Social worker
- Relationship therapist
- Insurance broker
- Gardener
- Midwife
- Museum worker
- Chef (you're known as the best cook in the zodiac!)
- Security guard
- Charity CEO
- PR consultant
- Beauty therapist

CANCER AT PLAY

No other sign is as affected by their own positive or negative thoughts and emotional states as you! When you're feeling happy, safe, and secure, you have loads of energy and all feels well with the world. When you're out of sorts, your sensitive digestive system can be the first to tell you that something's not right. Being near water relaxes you almost as much as swimming in it. A walk along a beach or a stroll by a river soothes you in a magical manner.

Food and drink

- You love traditional restaurants or a home-cooked family dinner.
- You are seen as a talented cook because you are willing to experiment.
- As a Water sign, drinking plenty of fluids keeps you feeling balanced.
- You tend to eat when you're feeling anxious, bored, or excited!

Get moving

You dislike aggressive forms of exercise and feeling uncomfortable, so getting sweaty and breathless isn't your thing. Gentler hobbies, such as yoga, walking, dancing, and swimming, keep you active and are more soothing for your nerves.

Leo

July 23–
August 23

ALL ABOUT LEO

SYMBOL: THE LION
ELEMENT: FIRE △
RULER: THE SUN

The constellation of Leo

Like the Sun, your place is at the heart of the solar system, where everything revolves around you! Everyone notices when a Leo saunters into a room. You're full of warmth and positivity—and you sparkle with life. You were born to lead the pack, to encourage, protect, and provide. Your motivation is usually to make other people happy, and yes, you can be a little bit firm in enforcing your rules sometimes … But you know you are strong and brave and that your intentions come from the heart.

Creative kick

When there's nobody around to watch you, you might as well be invisible! Try to take time out from others to find out who you really are. It won't take long for your creative instinct to kick in, and making something will give you a purpose—without needing an audience.

Something wonderful

Most Leos want to change the world for the better— and what better way than to make something beautiful? You were born with the talent and love to show off your skills. But for all your self-confidence, you do need encouragement. And when the praise comes, you prefer it to be as flattering as possible, preferably sung from the rooftops.

Kind counsel

You often find it easier to get others' lives in order, rather than concentrating on your own. Some of your friends and family may label this overeagerness to help as bossiness. But you'll argue that you're just pushing them to be the best they can. Besides, you're such a wise person that others will naturally come to you for advice anyway!

LEO AND RELATIONSHIPS

You don't find it difficult to show your affections, and you feel alive when you've just met someone new. You may hold back until you're sure you can win them over, but as soon as you get the slightest hint that they like you, too, you'll pounce! Grand romantic gestures don't get more dramatic than a Leo in love. Your crush will be bowled over—and perhaps a little overwhelmed. Few people find it easy to be as generous as you. Try and remember that love can be quiet and personal, without everything being for show.

Perfect relationships?

- You need to be adored! You love big gestures and public shows of affection.
- What other people think of the people you love is a big issue. You want your friends and partners to like each other.
- If your partner is happy to spend all day reading a book, you can feel ignored and alone. (Two emotions you're uncomfortable with!)
- You prefer to be with people who enjoy an exciting social scene—life's too short to stay at home.

GOOD MATCH
- Libra
- Sagittarius
- Gemini

STEER CLEAR
- Leo
- Scorpio
- Capricorn

LEO AT WORK

As one of the most creative and artistic signs of the zodiac, you only enjoy work in which you can express yourself. You are happiest when you can stand by your work and proudly declare, "I did that!" You excel in any position where the focus is on you. The entertainment industry has a magnetic pull for Leo looking for the limelight, and singing, dancing, or a career in music will be high on your list. Leo loves to take charge, making you a natural boss and a popular leader.

Inspirational Leo

- **Barack Obama—Politician**
- **Daniel Radcliffe—Actor**
- **Amelia Earhart—Aviator**
- **Demi Lovato—Singer and mental health advocate**
- **Neil Armstrong—Astronaut**

Ideal Leo careers

- Actor
- Influencer
- Fashion designer
- Circus ringmaster
- Cruise ship entertainer
- Opera singer
- Comedian
- Cardiologist

LEO AT PLAY

You're a high-energy person with a zest for life. You take exercise seriously, partly because you're a Fire sign, and feel more relaxed when you've burned off some energy. You would rather be outside in the fresh air than cooped up in a gym. Relaxing is a big deal for you, but even your downtime can look hectic to less energetic types. As the zodiac's party animal, you won't leave until the music stops! But lions need their sleep ... and you can get irritable if you haven't had time to lounge around for a few days.

Food and drink

- You'd love to be able to eat out all the time—you get to show off your outfit, talk to everyone, and be seen in a fashionable spot. Besides, washing the dishes isn't your thing.
- You love baking awesome-looking cakes because of the wow factor.
- When you choose from the menu, you usually look for most exciting options.
- You are a perfect dinner date. A generous lion, you often insist on paying!

Get moving

You can't keep a Lion indoors for long—unless they're sleeping. You're happiest when surrounded by other people, so being a member of a team will satisfy your social instincts. Soccer, basketball, field hockey, and other team sports will appeal, and of course, you aim to be the star player.

Virgo

August 24–
September 22

ALL ABOUT VIRGO

SYMBOL: THE MAIDEN
ELEMENT: EARTH ▽
RULER: MERCURY

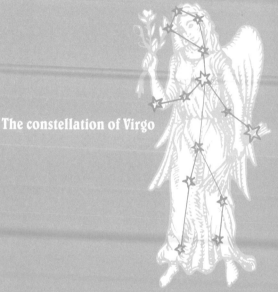

The constellation of Virgo

The Maiden is usually depicted holding sheaves of wheat, symbolizing the harvest in late summer—Virgo time. The wheat represents the wisdom she's gathered from different fields of experience. If anyone needs something done, they ask a Virgo first because they know they'll receive a sensible, practical answer that's beautifully simple. You were born to create order and keep things clean, polished, and organized.

Quietly amazing

You're not a huge fan of being in the spotlight, but once you get comfortable with the people around you, the communicative, Mercury-ruled side of your character appears. Your willingness to adjust makes people warm to you and listen to your advice. Even if you don't realize it, you're secretly the one in charge of everyone else in the zodiac.

Doing a good job

You're a hard worker with high standards. Modest to the core, you can be tough on yourself, and you like it when things are done properly! It's not that you really want to do all the work ... but it would irritate you too much to leave it to someone else who wouldn't do as good a job.

Clean and tidy

Your desire for perfection can sometimes mean that you spend a lot of time concentrating on things that aren't quite right. You probably have a very clean, tidy home, because you can't relax until you have order. After all, it's hard to write an email if your desk's a mess!

VIRGO AND RELATIONSHIPS

You're a naturally private person, so when you first realize you like someone, it can take you by surprise. You are picky, but that's just because you know what you're looking for. You're naturally shy—and will probably think of a hundred reasons why your crush won't be interested. But if you stand back and take an honest look at yourself, you will notice the charming, kind, and talented person everyone else sees. One of your greatest lessons is to accept your own failings … and those of others. Everyone is flawed and still lovable—even you!

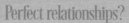

Perfect relationships?

- Your planetary ruler, Mercury, looks for friendship. Once in a relationship, you are committed.
- You want your life together to be private. You won't be happy if your friends and partners are always posting photos of you on social media.
- Honesty is key! Knowing what the people you love really think is far more important to you than being told what you want to hear.
- You notice all the little details about people, from where they buy their shoes to which toothpaste they prefer.

GOOD MATCH
- Pisces
- Virgo
- Taurus

STEER CLEAR
- Aries
- Sagittarius
- Libra

VIRGO AT WORK

You're a hard-working problem-solver, famed for your clear, uncluttered communication style. You like to look at the task in front of you piece by piece and analyze the information in detail. Your thoroughness is unique, and when given a job to do, you treat it seriously. It might take a little longer for you to complete a project than the other zodiac signs, because you will correct and adjust every single error as you go, but the end results will be perfect—no matter whether you're an accountant or a trombone player!

Inspirational Virgo

- **Zendaya—Actor**
- **Beyoncé—Musician**
- **Ava DuVernay—Director**
- **Lili Reinhart—Actor**
- **Mother Teresa—Missionary**
- **Roald Dahl—Writer**

Ideal Virgo careers

- Computer engineer
- Laboratory assistant
- Nutritionist
- Life coach
- Air traffic controller
- Journalist
- Veterinarian
- Accountant
- Restaurant critic
- Doctor
- Surgeon

VIRGO AT PLAY

Virgo is the zodiac sign most connected with health, habits, and routine. You don't get bored as easily as the other signs, so repetitive exercise keeps you happy. Activities such as hiking, distance running, and swimming will all help you feel energized. It can be hard for you to switch off the need to learn, improve, and be productive and just unwind. Sometimes, you're so busy looking after everyone else that you can't see that you're the one in need of a little TLC!

Food and drink

- As the zodiac sign most connected with digestion, you feel out of sorts when you're not eating properly.
- You're likely to be clued-up on nutrition and healthy eating, and junk food does not impress you.
- You may choose to be a vegan or vegetarian, and you always insist on the best-quality ingredients.
- It's easier for you to eat at home, since you can be picky at restaurants.

Get moving

You're all about progress. You love to stay active—mostly because you can see yourself getting better and better! Keeping logs of how fast you can run, how many goals you can score, or how many sets you can do can help you stay focused.

Libra

September 23–
October 22

ALL ABOUT LIBRA

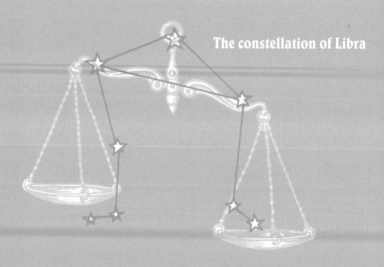

The constellation of Libra

You're one of the most sociable signs of the zodiac, but your desire to please others means that you sometimes sacrifice your own ambitions to keep the peace. Since you are the sign of balance—and an excellent listener—you like to hear all sides of a story before deciding on the fairest course of action. It can take you a long time to weigh up all the options, but when you do make a decision, it's usually set in stone (unless too many people disagree with you!).

Others' opinions

You were born to discuss your thoughts and feelings with others. It's natural for you to think about others' opinions before you make up your own mind—even if you don't agree with them. You see yourself through the eyes of other people, so their good opinion of you helps you form a good opinion of yourself.

Venusian beauty

You have a deep appreciation for beauty and are quite particular about how you decorate your environment and yourself. Style is more important than comfort in your eyes, and you'll pick beautiful shoes over practical ones every time. Your ideal home is a clutter-free, peaceful space, decorated with flowers, candles, and works of art.

Moral maze

You are a tolerant person who hates to make a scene. Always giving people the benefit of the doubt is admirable— as long as you are dealing with people who have equally high morals. Lesser individuals can become frustrated with your passivity and try to provoke you into making decisions.

LIBRA AND RELATIONSHIPS

Libra is the sign of partnership, and you love the drama of romance. You believe in finding your soulmate, but you might take a long time to make up your mind about what you are looking for. (It's too important a decision to make quickly!) Luckily, your sociable personality and awesome smile make sure you're never short of friends. You feel unsettled by anger, chaos, and noise, and you stay away from fights. If you argue with someone, you probably try and make the peace as quickly as possible—even if you're not in the wrong.

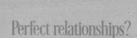

Perfect relationships?

- The excitement of a new romance is your idea of heaven.
- As a chatty Air sign, you get a kick out of sending messages back and forth.
- People have to appeal to your mind before you get truly hooked. You must feel that you're an equal partner in any relationship.
- You are very sensitive to criticisms and often worry about what people really think.

GOOD MATCH
- Gemini
- Aquarius
- Leo

STEER CLEAR
- Cancer
- Capricorn
- Virgo

LIBRA AT WORK

Behind your sweet, sociable personality lies a big business brain. As one of the zodiac's communicators, you understand how to persuade people to work together. You're a friendly, chilled, and witty character, and surprisingly cool and logical when faced with stressful tasks. You make a very amiable, sociable leader, although you are not altogether comfortable being the one making all the decisions. Some may say friendliness gets in the way of work, but for you, the opposite is usually true. When you need something done, the people around you are happy to help.

Inspirational Libra

- **Alexandria Ocasio-Cortez—Politician**
- **Mae Jemison—Astronaut**
- **Mahatma Gandhi—Politician**
- **Anthony Mackie—Actor**
- **Doja Cat—Musician**
- **Naomi Osaka—Tennis player**

Ideal Libra careers

- Human resources
- Relationship advisor
- Web designer
- Makeup artist
- Fashion designer
- Public relations consultant
- Hairdresser
- Art dealer
- Wedding planner
- Lawyer

LIBRA AT PLAY

Venus-ruled signs are usually well-groomed and spend a great deal of care on their appearance, so getting hot, sweaty, and breathless won't be your first choice when it comes to staying active. To relax and unwind, chatting with friends is your preferred way to chill. Talking out any problems and knowing that someone else understands where you're coming from is the best therapy. Therapy can also work wonderfully well if you wish to express what's on your mind without worrying about saying what you really feel.

Food and drink

- Your ruler, Venus, is the planet of enjoyment, and good food is usually a high priority.
- Balance is the key to Libra's health and well-being—and that includes a balanced diet,
- You like to keep your food choices interesting, but you dislike rich food because it saps your energy.
- Libra's sensitive skin will quickly show the effects of lack of sleep or water. So stay hydrated!

Get moving

The gym doesn't hold much appeal for you—unless it's a cool place to hang out, in which case you'll enjoy spending time in the cafe, chatting to friends over lunch! Tennis and badminton, or any sports or activity requiring a partner, will suit your need to work with someone else, so ballroom dancing, Zumba, and water-fitness classes appeal, too.

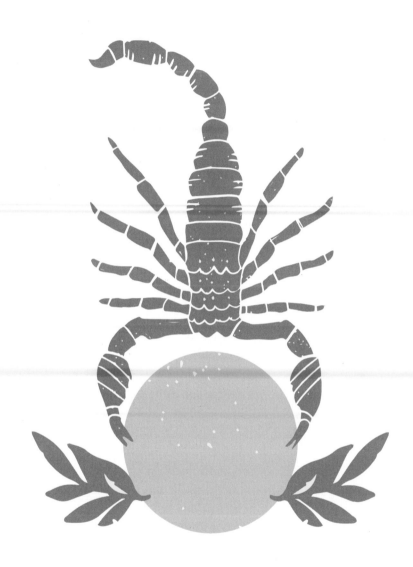

Scorpio

October 23–
November 21

ALL ABOUT SCORPIO

SYMBOL: THE SCORPION
ELEMENT: WATER ▽
RULER: PLUTO

The constellation of Scorpio

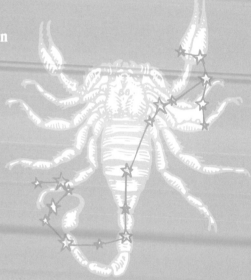

Hypnotic and mysterious with a sting in your tail, you are famous for having all the zodiac's most extreme and exciting personality traits. Like a scorpion, you prefer to hide yourself and keep your motives secret, but you will strike if you are threatened. Your tough exterior is there to protect your sensitive heart. You feel your emotions very deeply, but you won't let anyone see that you are vulnerable.

Keeping trust

You are great at keeping secrets because knowledge is power! Trust is everything to you. That's why you rely on so few people yourself. You'll enjoy hearing gossip as much as anyone, but you treat real secrets with the respect they deserve ... and you have a few of your own.

The power of money

Scorpio is one of the financial zodiac signs. Ruled by the planet Pluto, you respect the power of money, and your relationship with it can be complicated. You're smart and shrewd, and you tend to find that money comes to you easily ... but you're quite secretive about how much money you have!

Losing yourself

When you get interested in a subject, idea, or character, you become very obsessive. You're the kind of person who binge-watches TV series, or you stay up all night reading an absorbing story.

SCORPIO AND RELATIONSHIPS

As the zodiac's most passionate sign, your intensity can make people feel a little uncomfortable, but it's not intentional. You take love seriously and don't make it easy for others to get close, but when you find true love, you are loyal, protective, and caring. Emotionally, you give everything, so if someone behaves in a way that hurts you, you will want revenge. (Remember that the best revenge of all is to find a way not to care!) Because you are brave and honest with yourself, you have the power to heal and put yourself back together stronger than before.

Perfect relationships?

- When you really like someone, you may try to keep your feelings to yourself, but your eyes will give you away.
- You can't help noticing all the details of the people you love, such as the way they move and the sound of their voice.
- You can become possessive of your partner and feel jealous if provoked.
- Scorpio needs to be the one and only. If you have any doubt, they will know—and they won't be happy!

GOOD MATCH
- Cancer
- Taurus
- Capricorn

STEER CLEAR
- Libra
- Leo
- Aries

SCORPIO AT WORK

Any work for which you have to dig deep to discover more information will suit your detective brain. You love getting to the heart of what really motivates people. There's no problem you can't solve, and you demand respect without ever asking for it. You give away little about your own life, yet you miss nothing about what other people do. If you see something wrong, you don't always make a big deal at the time ... but you'll remember the details in case that information comes in handy at a later date.

Inspirational Scorpio

- Marie Curie—Scientist
- Katy Perry—Musician
- Pablo Picasso—Artist
- Willow Smith—Musician
- Amandla Stenberg—Actor
- Bill Gates—Entrepreneur

Ideal Scorpio careers

- Negotiator
- Spy
- Detective
- Tax consultant
- Police officer
- Event planner
- Researcher
- Psychologist
- Miner
- Investment banker

SCORPIO AT PLAY

Your calm exterior hides your intense nature. One of the most important things you can do for your health is to talk to someone about your feelings. You have such a rich emotional life but keep things very much to yourself—and keeping things in can lead to bigger problems. Scorpio loves a ritual, so if you're feeling down, soothe yourself by lighting a candle, making a mug of hot chocolate, and putting on a great track. You adore music, and listening to it can boost your mood like nothing else.

Food and drink

- You tend to enjoy foods that other people find a bit too much—for example, very sweet, bitter, or spicy.
- You can swing from being obsessed with one type of food to shunning it completely a few days later.
- You have no problem sticking to a healthy eating plan for a short time ... then you shoot the other way and want nothing but takeouts!
- Beware of fad diets! Healthy eating is all about balance.

Get moving

You're driven, energetic, and competitive. Extreme sports such as rock climbing, skiing, cave diving, and kite surfing will help you relieve stress and help move any blocked energy.

Sagittarius
November 22–
December 19

ALL ABOUT SAGITTARIUS

SYMBOL: THE ARCHER
ELEMENT: FIRE △
RULER: JUPITER

**The constellation
of Sagittarius**

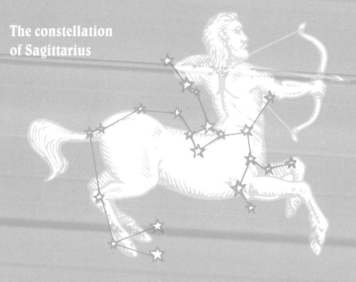

Your astrological symbol is the Archer, usually shown as a centaur—a mythological creature, half man, half horse. Legend has it that you would shoot your arrow, gallop to where it landed, then shoot again—covering the entire globe and delighting in every new experience. You love to travel and are always ready to explore new places and meet new people. You live for adventure and tackle life's challenges with a smile on your face.

Keep moving

You're at your happiest at the beginning of a new project. Your enthusiasm moves you forward with tremendous force. Your energy is more rough and ready than thoughtful and refined, but the sheer optimism you apply to everything can be very refreshing.

Independent thinker

Philosophical matters fascinate you. You don't like being told what to believe in or how to live by anyone—teachers, friends, family, or the government. You enjoy a good verbal battle with anyone who disagrees with you, but it drives you crazy when people challenge your intelligence. You've studied hard and explored the world, and you feel you have put in the work to be right!

Spend, spend, spend

Hating to be restricted, especially when it comes to fun, you cheerfully spend money as quickly as you get it. It's good that your ruler Jupiter is the luckiest planet of all! Just when you're down to your last coins, your fortunes can change, and you're back in the black again.

SAGITTARIUS AND RELATIONSHIPS

You are a creature of contradictions, and love can tear you in two directions. You value your freedom very deeply, so thinking that you may really care about someone can bring mixed feelings. However, once you are committed, you want to share your whole world with the people you care about and experience life's adventures all together. As the zodiac's "truth seeker," you are always honest. Your truths tend to be delivered bluntly, and you may even break a few hearts along the way ...

Perfect relationships?

- Big on jokes, puns, and generally playing the fool, you are hard to ignore.
- Your optimism and enormous appetite for life is catching, and helps you win over the coldest hearts!
- A staid, comfortable kind of love doesn't appeal —you prefer something a bit more challenging.
- Extremely generous in love, you expect only one thing in return—one hundred percent honesty.

GOOD MATCH
- Leo
- Libra
- Gemini

STEER CLEAR
- Scorpio
- Cancer
- Virgo

SAGITTARIUS AT WORK

Everyone needs an optimistic, enterprising Sagittarian on their team! Your belief in yourself and willingness to take on any challenge carries everyone forward. However, you can lose interest over the less exciting aspects of a job, such as budgeting or planning. A contradictory character, there are usually two kinds of Sagittarians—academics or athletic types. Whichever one you are, you need a career that will satisfy your thirst for knowledge. You are happier being the boss than following orders.

Inspirational Sagittarius

- **Janelle Monáe—Musician**
- **Taylor Swift—Musician**
- **Jane Austen—Writer**
- **Billie Eilish—Musician**
- **Walt Disney—Film Producer**
- **Hailee Steinfeld—Actor and musician**

Ideal Sagittarius careers

- Travel agent
- Salesperson
- Sports coach
- Entrepreneur
- Teacher
- Theologian
- Overseas aid worker
- Spiritual guru
- Politician
- Explorer

SAGITTARIUS AT PLAY

If you're a sporty Sagittarian, you'll be strong, energetic, and competitive. You're naturally speedy, love a challenge, and have complete faith in your abilities. An excellent teacher, you enjoy encouraging others to achieve their best. If you're more of a thoughtful Sagittarian, you may be less interested in exercise and more into books. Luckily, almost all Sagittarians love walking because it satisfies your curiosity to see what's around the next corner.

Food and drink

- You're a quantity rather than quality person—a shopper who visits the supermarket over a specialist grocer.
- Imagine a medieval banquet with a huge table creaking with all kinds of food—that's your kind of dinner!
- You like to have well-stocked cupboards ... in case your friends come over for a surprise party.
- Your love of travel means that some of your best-loved foods are things you've tried on vacation.

Get moving

Athletics and team games help you burn off energy and are great for your competitive nature. Hiking, rock climbing, and sailing all appeal to your love of the outdoors, and should prove exciting enough to hold your attention.

Capricorn
December 20– January 19

ALL ABOUT CAPRICORN

SYMBOL: THE GOAT
ELEMENT: EARTH △
RULING PLANET: SATURN

You are a realistic, practical, and hard-working person—the most ambitious character in the zodiac. Capricorn's symbol is the Goat, sometimes drawn as a mythical sea goat. It represents your determination to reach the top in everything you do. As an Earth sign, you trust in what you can see, touch, and build, and you expect to work hard to achieve success. You may be uncomfortable expressing more complicated feelings until you are a little older.

Clever with money

With a mature head on your shoulders, you're not about to waste the money you put so much time and energy into creating. One of the main reasons you're such a financial whiz is that you have a plan and you stick to it. (Surprisingly few people have the discipline to plod through tasks in quite the same way as Capricorn!)

Sweet and stylish

You have excellent taste and want to look and sound like you mean business. You have something of a formal manner and conservative appearance. Dressed to impress in timeless fashions and tasteful accessories, you bring an air of sophistication wherever you go.

Forever climbing

Your drive, knowledge, and sheer hard work will propel you to the top of your chosen game, and that's naturally where you feel most confident and secure. You are happy being the person who makes all the important decisions, and romance may take a back seat while you concentrate on your career.

CAPRICORN AND RELATIONSHIPS

As one of the most practical Earth signs of the zodiac, you don't shout about your feelings—at least, not until you've thoroughly checked out your crush on social media. You long to meet someone you can share your life with and since you're attractive, wise, and funny, you won't have too much trouble. You keep your feelings private until you feel safe, but when you do meet someone suitable, you don't treat it lightly. The people who really matter will see the loving, passionate side of you that the rest of the word rarely does.

Perfect relationships?

- The start of a relationship can be overwhelming; you're more comfortable when things settle down.
- You don't expect sunshine and rainbows all the time. You understand that nobody is perfect—including yourself.
- You may prefer the more conventional model for love—getting married, buying a home, and having children.
- You will be devoted to making your relationships work and enjoy setting goals for yourself as a friend or partner.

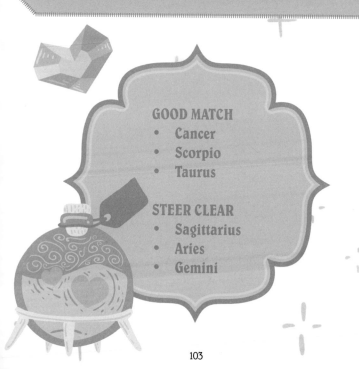

GOOD MATCH
- Cancer
- Scorpio
- Taurus

STEER CLEAR
- Sagittarius
- Aries
- Gemini

CAPRICORN AT WORK

You are the hardest worker of the zodiac, and if you haven't already achieved something impressive, you'll be slowly working your way toward it. After all, reaching the top is what you naturally want to do. You'll never tell your boss that something can't be done—you'll find a way even if it means learning a whole new set of skills. When you get to be the boss, you're right where you ought to be! Firm but fair, you reward loyalty, but if anyone tries to deceive you, you're not amused.

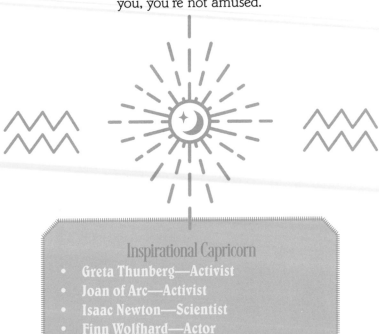

Inspirational Capricorn

- Greta Thunberg—Activist
- Joan of Arc—Activist
- Isaac Newton—Scientist
- Finn Wolfhard—Actor
- Michelle Obama—Lawyer
- Dove Cameron—Actor

Ideal Capricorn careers

- Politician
- Accountant
- Legal secretary
- Salesperson
- Town planner
- Mortgage advisor
- Lecturer
- Entrepreneur
- Business analyst
- Architect

CAPRICORN AT PLAY

You want to be the best at whatever you are doing. Be careful not to push yourself too hard! Getting enough fresh air and daylight is vital for Earth signs to keep healthy and vibrant. A brisk walk and a good night's sleep will help you unwind and focus on something other than work. You need to make time to be kind to yourself, since you get self-critical when you feel you're not getting enough done.

Food and drink

- You have lots of self-control when it comes to food and are quick to choose healthy eating habits.
- Most of the time, you find it easy to eat regularly, but if you're working too hard, food gets forgotten!
- A kitchen is often where Capricorn feels most secure, and you love to cook foods filled with fire and spice.
- Sometimes you like one food so much that you find yourself eating it day after day after day …

Get moving

You have a strong constitution and find it easy to stick to an exercise regime. As a Goat, climbing will be an obvious activity choice, but any form of exercise during which you steadily work toward success is good. You have the stamina for long-distance running, and the grace and poise to be an elegant ice skater or gymnast.

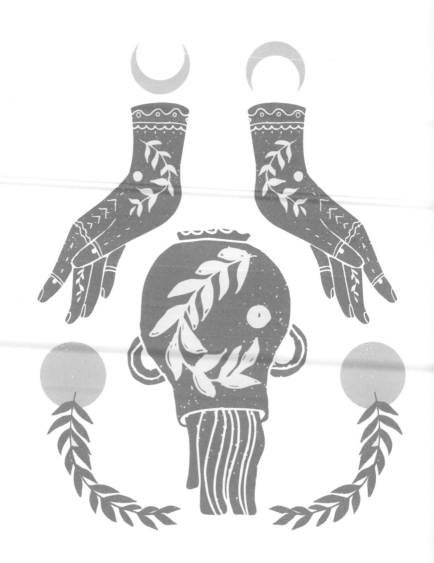

Aquarius

January 20– February 19

ALL ABOUT AQUARIUS

SYMBOL: THE WATER CARRIER
ELEMENT: AIR ▽
RULER: URANUS

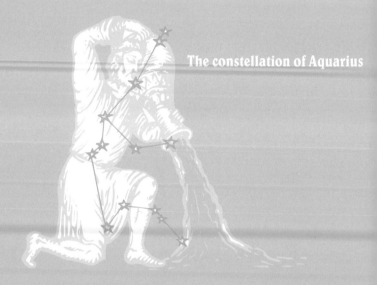

The constellation of Aquarius

The astrological symbol for Aquarius is the Water Carrier, usually shown as a man pouring water from a pitcher. This can make people think that Aquarius is a Water sign, but it is not—you're an idealistic Air sign, and you spend more time in your head than any other sign of the zodiac. You are a friendly, inventive, exciting person who is often described as unpredictable. You're not keen on tradition and long for a more tolerant and diverse vision of society.

Big mystery

Mysterious subjects, such as ancient religions and conspiracy theories, inspire and excite you. You're known for your unusual tastes and style, and if everyone else is becoming interested in something, the chances are you'll have done it months ago!

Follow your own rules

You can appear distant or distracted because you don't always connect with people on an emotional level. But you're sharp as a tack, perhaps even more so when you're concentrating on something really interesting.

Weirdly stubborn

Once you have decided that you're right about something, there is no other explanation available. You're extremely clever, but you believe in your own logic. Aquarius is full of contradictions, and although you are open-minded about many things, when it comes to your own personal actions, you will not budge.

AQUARIUS AND RELATIONSHIPS

You're deeply curious about other people, and if you're with someone, you will ask lots of questions to find out everything you can about them. However, you're a free spirit and often find that you can hop from an obsession with one person to another without much trouble. Cool and glamorous, you have an air of mystery, which means you're never short of friends. But for you to get really hooked on someone, they have to intrigue you ...

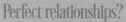

Perfect relationships?

- You tend to love in a gentle, eternally friendly, way and have an almost scientific interest in the people you care about.
- You're a logical creature, and true love can be a difficult concept for you to get your head around.
- You're often embarrassed by emotions, and you'll do your best to keep your own hidden.
- When one person means everything to you, you'll be confused but excited. After all, it's a new experience!

GOOD MATCH
- Libra
- Leo
- Aquarius

STEER CLEAR
- Taurus
- Scorpio
- Cancer

AQUARIUS AT WORK

It may take you a little while before you find a career that will keep you interested. You're happy to explore until you find something that doesn't make you bored. It's never all about the money for Aquarius—it's about ripping up old traditions that are no longer working and replacing them with brilliant new ideas that will revolutionize the planet! You seem to have a radar that points out how to improve people's lives with your original solutions.

Inspirational Aquarius

- **Rosa Parks—Activist**
- **Harry Styles—Musician and actor**
- **Elizabeth Olsen—Actor**
- **Buzz Aldrin—Astronaut**
- **Michael B. Jordan—Actor**
- **Charles Darwin—Scientist**

Ideal Aquarius careers

- Scientist
- Politician
- Professor
- Computer programmer
- Engineer
- Air traffic controller
- Astrologer
- Social enterprise professional
- Alternative therapist
- Inventor

AQUARIUS AT PLAY

It can be hard for you to get really motivated about moving your body because it can take you away from what you're really interested in—long nights staring at your computer or using all your energy trying to solve a scientific puzzle. Naturally rebellious, you'll question traditional advice and prefer to do your own research. If there's a theory that fits with your current ideas about diet and exercise, you'll try it.

Food and drink

- You have a good understanding of the need for balance and variety in food, and enjoy planning meals in advance.
- You have a progressive attitude and may be drawn to vegan or vegetarian meals.
- Forget simple meals—you're usually more interested in unusual vegetables and protein bars designed for astronauts.
- You're an unpredictable eater, and anything too samey drives you crazy.

Get moving

Exercise isn't something you like to schedule. You get bored with any repetitive physical movement—and going to the same gym at the same time every day won't appeal much. As an extroverted, social sign of the zodiac, being around others lifts your spirits and fills you with energy, so team sports and busy classes are more fulfilling.

Pisces
February 20–
March 20

ALL ABOUT PISCES

SYMBOL: THE FISH
ELEMENT: WATER ▽
RULER: NEPTUNE

**The constellation
of Pisces**

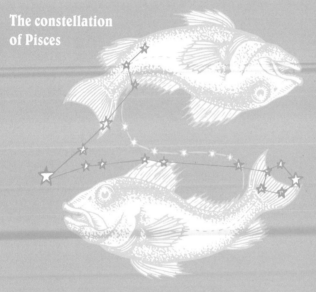

You are the most compassionate and spiritual of all the zodiac signs, with a sensitive nature and amazing imagination. As a deeply emotional Water sign, you might find that you sometimes get swept away on waves of feeling. You are ruled by Neptune, the planet of magic and illusion, and have a reputation for being wonderfully creative. You know real beauty when you find it—and you have the ability to bring happiness to others through just being yourself.

Powerhouse of talent

Your sensitivity allows creativity to stream through you, and you're never happier than when you're in full flow. You may not feel a strong desire to get your ideas and creations out into the world for others to see, but you're capable of producing the most amazing pieces of music, poetry, and art.

The meaning of money

You either see money as the root of all evil or as something that just cascades through you like water through a strainer. One problem is that you can't say no to people in trouble. You'll see one sad-looking dog and give all the cash you have to an animal shelter!

Don't give yourself away

You're a wonderful listener and often find yourself hearing about other people's secrets, worries, and woes. This means that it's important that you get time on your own to recover your sense of self. Otherwise, it can be hard to separate your own thoughts and feelings from those of others.

PISCES AND RELATIONSHIPS

Your symbol is two fish swimming in opposite directions. This represents the way that you can easily flip between fantasy and reality. You're in love with love and feel sure that one day you will meet the perfect person. Sometimes, you project what you so badly want onto other people, that you'll make yourself believe it's true. When you're let down, you hurt like nobody else, but because you allow yourself to feel so much, you are great at processing your feelings and moving on.

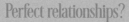

Perfect relationships?

- The idea of love is so tempting that you can swim from one person to another in search of "the one."
- Honesty is what you need most from others, but it's not always easy for you to hear the truth.
- You find magic in sadness—and may be drawn to people who have faced real difficulties.
- A pretty weed growing through a crack in the road can fill your heart with joy, and a smile from a stranger in a store instantly restores your faith in humanity.

GOOD MATCH
- Scorpio
- Virgo
- Cancer

STEER CLEAR
- Aries
- Gemini
- Leo

PISCES AT WORK

You absorb the atmosphere of the pond you swim in, so your working environment is important to you. You may spend a few years moving from place to place, as you try to discover somewhere that pushes all the right buttons. You prefer a job that involves working quietly in the background. This means that you sometimes surprise people with your imaginative ideas. You're the artist of the zodiac and express yourself through painting, music, pottery, writing, or fashion. You're not too tempted by responsibility and are happy to let others take the lead.

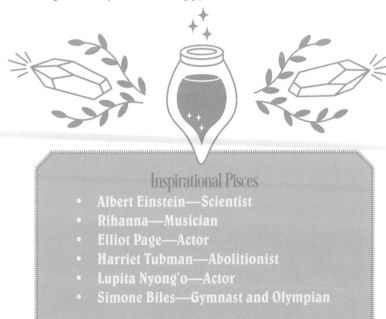

Inspirational Pisces

- **Albert Einstein—Scientist**
- **Rihanna—Musician**
- **Elliot Page—Actor**
- **Harriet Tubman—Abolitionist**
- **Lupita Nyong'o—Actor**
- **Simone Biles—Gymnast and Olympian**

Ideal Pisces careers
- Artist
- Charity fundraiser
- Chemist
- Actor
- Dancer
- Nurse
- Psychologist
- Priest
- Swimmer
- Chiropodist

PISCES AT PLAY

Like a fish swimming through water, you're an elegant, gliding mover. You usually exist inside your imagination, and health issues are often caused by emotional stress. As a Water sign, you might find that you easily pick up negativity from others. You tend to spend a lot of time worrying if you don't feel well and imagine problems to be greater than they are. Naturally restless, you are more interested in trying lots of different things than sticking to a strict exercise regime.

Food and drink

- You can be indecisive—you don't know what you want to eat and prefer others to choose.
- Many Pisceans find they prefer a vegetarian diet.
- You may be picky about food, but you need lots of vitamins and minerals to keep your immune system strong.
- If you're feeling stressed, you may find yourself turning to food to help you feel better.

Get moving

Dancing is a much-loved activity because it's linked with the feet—the Piscean area of the body. You might feel self-conscious exercising in a group, so going it alone at home or joining an internet class (with your camera off) can keep things more private. You're in your element in the water, and going for a quick dip in the ocean or a lake is sure to be bliss!

"THOSE WHO DON'T BELIEVE IN MAGIC WILL NEVER FIND IT."

ROALD DAHL

Other titles in the series:
Spells * Crystals * Palm Reading *
Divination * Manifesting * Tarot

The Teen Witches' Guide to

Astrology

Written by Xanna Eve Chown
and Marion Williamson

Illustrated by Luna Valentine

ARCTURUS

This edition published in 2024 by Arcturus Publishing Limited
26/27 Bickels Yard, 151–153 Bermondsey Street, London SE1 3HA

Writers: Xanna Eve Chown and Marion Williamson
Illustrator: Luna Valentine
Designer: Rosie Bellwood
Editor: Donna Gregory

ISBN: 978-1-3988-1517-9
CH010260NT
Supplier 29, Date 0324, PI 00006547

Printed in China